# The Evolution of I

# The Evolution Of I

## PIMP Publications

### Illustrations by Kennedie Caples

# **<u>Dedication</u>**

*I want to thank God for the opportunity, the journey, the trials, and the tribulations. They truly made me who I am today. As a young artist, I am blessed to have gained this talent. It took me a very long time to see the true potential I have for myself. I chose to give it to God and walk by faith, and I thank you Lord for this first step.*

# PIMP's Prelude

*Before I was PIMP, I was a short kid who got bullied and never knew how to speak up. Days spent with depression and built-up anger. Never knowing if I was doing anything wrong led me through a long battle of self-identity. People all my life tried to belittle me, push me out, silence me, and underestimated me. Through poetry I learned how to speak up for myself. As I learned poetry, I learned myself.*

# _PIMP's Prelude Pt. II_

_Through all the rain and the pain,_
_It wasn't the fame I wanted to gain,_
_I wanted respect instead of vain._
_So, within this name,_
_I hope that's what I'll obtain._


**_-Picture In My Perspective_**

# Table Of Contents

## 9th Grade

- Through the Night
- Heavy Heart
- Bitter Bliss
- Open Casket

## 10th Grade

- Forced Cocoon
- Living on the Fence
- Third Person View
- Rose within Cement

## 11th Grade

- Hometown
- A Sinner's Cry
- Madness
- Indecisive Art
- School
- Ode to Old I

## 12<sup>th</sup> Grade

- Higher Self
- Park Prayer
- Recognition
- 1%
- Congratulations

## Post-Graduation

- Path of Righteousness
- Poetic Journey
- Dear Mom
- 1/3
- LLC
- River Rock
- On a Come Up

# 9<sup>th</sup> Grade

# Through the Night

In the nighttime.
Where I'm hard to find.
Where I'm so divine.
On a thin line.
Might cave in.
Might blow over.
Might go under.
Every day I try to be the best of
me.
Y'all mess with me,
Might get the worst of me.
Might make you bleed.
Turn into a killer fiend.
You are not a friend of me.
Yes, nigga I'm your enemy.
You're dead to me.
My anger is like soda.
You shook it up and threw me.
Now you are scared.
Now you shake.
Now you gonna panic.

Now you quick to can it.
You say, "Where's the real Zay."
I say "he ain't on this planet."

# Heavy Heart

My heart is feeling heavy,
But it's not from heart break. It's
from all the pain that's thrown at
me.
How much more can I take?
Every second I breathe.
I feel like I'm a mistake.
Should I erase?
Happiness is getting harder and
harder to chase.
All these burdens on my chest,
Weighing me down like breasts.
I can't escape the pain.
I'm under their restraints.
Mind going blurry,
Can't stay in my lane.
I'm locked up like I'm under
arrest.

I'm screaming for help at
someone who's higher in power.
I feel like I disappointed Him
too.

I wish I can be blessed like i said
"achoo"

## Bitter Bliss

Sometimes I just want to go over,
And stop my whole existence.
Because every time I feel happy,
There's always some resistance.
You said you're here for me,
That's too far of a distance.
When you listen,
I shut you out so what's the
difference.
I'm on a mission,
I'm sorry if I come off as vicious.
When I'm away,
I ain't doing nun suspicious.
I'm just in my own world,
Stuck in a reminiscence.

# Open Casket

Can you see the pain hidden in
my eyes?
They scream for help,
Every time I cry.
It leaves a stream that trails
nearby.
You know my past,
Why would you still lie?
So don't open up to me.
In my open casket,
You see,
Surrounded by poems and love
letters from me to thee.
Placed by my loved ones,
Who loved something unique
about me.
Most importantly,
How I was once a shy boy who
taught himself how to speak.

Taught himself he's worthy.
Staying up late nights.
Feelings of worry and dirty,
Laying in debris,
Thinking about his future,
Can't seem to make it past thirty.
Ladies and gentlemen,
This isn't a scrape on the knee
This boy took his own life
Trying hard to live bougie
Old days wearing collared
Coogi
Short black boy who loves to
boogie
Lost his battle to the man named
Boogey

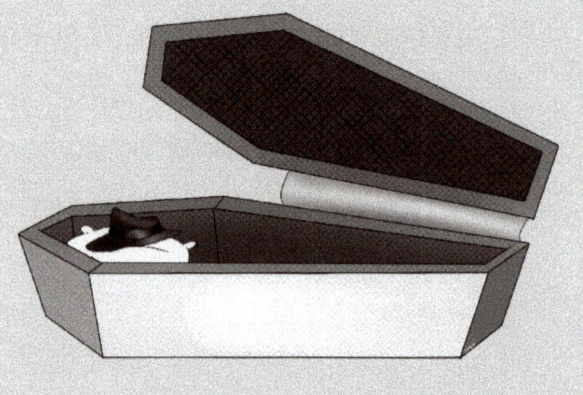

# 10<sup>th</sup> Grade

# Forced Cocoon

(Bottom-Top Poem)

Has been sucked into society.
The nice kid everyone once
knew,
Because the people are cruel.
They call it a cruel world.
Because people call you soft.
You can't be nice anymore,
In everything you do.
Where you always have to
compete.
What kind of world do we live
in?
Teachers loved him.
Cheered everyone up.
Making people laugh,
Always smiling,
He was nice as a kid.
That people brought.
Numb to the pain,
He had to become cold hearted.
He had to adapt.

In order to fit in.
The rudeness.
Away from all the negativity.
Below the world.
He casted in the shadows.

# Living On the Fence

In the nighttime,
Where it all goes down.
Everything turns around.
Everything goes all down.
Staring at the cold hard ground.
Thinking where it all went
wrong.
Wonder if I can make it out
strong.
I wonder has it been too long.
Standing on this side,
Knowing how many times
I've sat and cried.
I wonder should I cross this
fence.
Feeling all this suspense,
My heart feels dense.
Everything feels intense.

All I can do is sit back and wince.
Knowing that I'm living on the fence.

# Third Person View

It feels like I don't know who I
am anymore.
At one point.
I'm at a high,
Next, I'm at a low.
I'm getting aggressive,
I can't control.
People say the name "Zay"
It's like it doesn't belong to me.
just like this life,
I'm on the outside looking in.
I'm trapped within.
All these demons trying to take
over.
Can you hear my cry for help?
If I don't show it all the time,
I'm sorry.
I don't know how to project.
The more they come in.
The more I go.
Reach in and save me.
Before there is no hope.

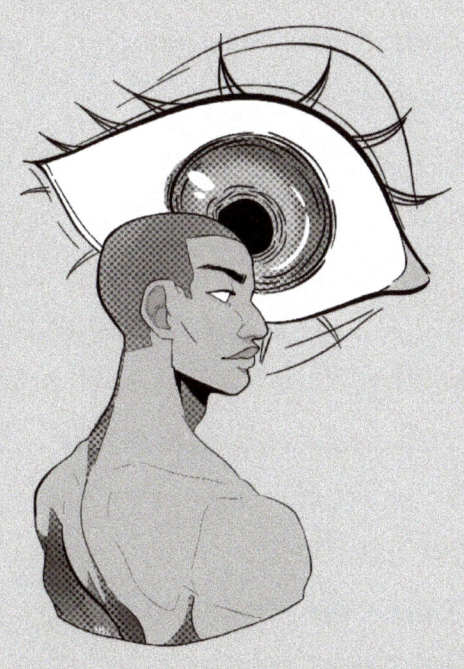

# Rose within Cement

I am a rose.
As you see.
I grew up nice and pretty.
I was always picked,
Always loved,
And everybody wants to see
me.
I spread joy to others,
Smile and happiness appear.
Again I say "what a good year"
Until my time has come.
I'm wilted,
I'm bruised,
I've been stepped on,
I've been trampled,
I've been worn out,
I've been abused.
I'm not as pretty as I was.
No one showed me love.
I wasn't noticed.

So as I been submerged into the
soil.
I start to distance myself.
Make my own world.
As I stay down here in the
Underground,
I'll know how it is to have no one
around.
As I carry on in this new life,
I don't want help from no other.
Down here I will sprout,
Only I can see the light but can't
no other.

# 11<sup>th</sup> Grade

## Hometown

I'm from a town where
Power lines were the coat racks,
And shoes were the hangers.
The people were the thumb
tacks,
And the children were the
bangers.
Forced to go to school with their
built up anger.
Just to come home and get
straight to slangin'.
9's and dimes,
Friends from my past times,
Facing hard time,
For doing big crimes,
Just to get their ma out the
grime.
Thank God that He picked mine.
Now I'm in the "Friendly City"
Still unsatisfied.
Cause my friends aren't with me.

Stuck in a town with no
opportunity.
Feeling shitty,
Don't worry.
Imma put us on the map like a
train filled with graffiti.
Tired of eating food that's meant
for the needy.
Mama, imma make sure I make
it on TV.
And give you all your wishes,
Like Queen Nefertiti.
Late night,
Eating leftover ziti.
Contemplating,
Will I make it where I wanna be?

## A Sinner's Cry

Lord, I just want to thank you,
Without having a reason why.
I want to thank You for looking
out for me.
All those times I lied to my mom
where I'm boutta be.

Thank You for all the food I
didn't say grace upon.
There were times I was hungry
and didn't eat all day long.

Lord, you saved me from the
mess.
All those days I was locked in
stress.
Head spinning,
I was walking around with a
rock in my chest.

Got lost and found myself,
stranded out west.
I can't do it without you.
I must confess,
I was the sheep that got away
from the rest.

# Madness

*(To The Tune of Thank You-Dido)*

My mind starts racing.
Can't think now,
Intrusive thought,
After thought,
And thought.
Just woke up five minutes ago.
I wish I was still at rest.
And even if I was,
It would all be mad.
I've seen my brother die.
It reminds me,
That my sleep is bad,
Hold my pain in my back.

## Indecisive Art

I got to get this idea in.
Jot it down,
Have it circled in blue pen.
Before my thoughts start to fuck
up the blueprint.
Try to run out the race,
I'm in the last sprint.
These rhymes come out of
nowhere.
Call it pocket lint.
I ask God is this my calling?
Take a hint.
Fuck it isn't.
I say I'm the best.
I really don't mean it.
I just had shit on my chest,
And I couldn't vent it.
So I had to put it in text.
It started from
Depressed,

Distressed,
How I feel in this mess,
I chose to confess,
So I put my words to the test.
I sent it out west,
And hella folks got impressed.
I'm truly blessed.
People desire the pain I congest.

## School

School is not the same as it used
to be,
When I was younger.
It was a home away from home.
I had fun,
I had friends,
I had great memories.
Until my friends became my
enemies.
Until all the joy and happiness
was stripped away from me.
I'm locked up for six hours,
Like I committed a felony.
Wardens all around,
Stressin' me.
I can't focus.
I'm trying so hard just to get the

bonus.
Points on the board and I have
the lowest.
I'm at my lowest.
I'm skipping class,
To look out the glass.
Wishing I was out,
Stepping on the grass.

## Ode to Ole I

This is for the new beginning,
With the same old feelings.
Transforming from my youth
Like a Mogwai to a gremlin.
I still remember all my days
I used to be stealing.
Walking thru Walmart,
Peeping the Ceiling.
Any cameras that may be in
vision?
Leave no evidence,
Nothing found or missing,
Use it for a while.
Sell it,
For commission.
Mama asks me why her stuff
came up missing?
Afraid to tell her that my pockets
were itchin'.
Thoughts in my head,
She could've spent it in the
kitchen.
But Shi

It feels like lynchin,
Sacrificing the opportunity
To get skrilla.
How am I supposed to get rich
and buy my mama dinner?
Even if I gotta risk losing,
To be a winner
Lord, please forgive me.
I know that I am a sinner.
Money just brings me peace,
From the inner.
But now I just wanna collect
and invest.
Get checks,
Flip it.
To match the next.
I hate to flex.
My new vision can now see the
specs.
My only regret,
Why is my mind so complex?
Deep breath for a sec,
Only way I cope with stress.
Pray for the best.
I do believe life's truly a test.

Not like the rest.
99% just pest.
Flies everywhere,
Gotta swat them to death.
This shit just flows.
At times I have a dam in my chest.
Baby bird of the flock,
Boutta fly from the nest.
Can't wait 'til I press.
"Mama, I made it" text.

# 12<sup>th</sup> Grade

# **<u>Higher Self</u>**

I inhale.
Through my stomach,
I can't feel my lungs.

## Park Prayer

Dark bark.
Electric spark.
Mosaic waves.
Scatter across my vision.
Creating a haze,
Allows me to envision.
Better days.
Leave me puzzled.
Trying to find ways,
To make it out this normal life.
Such a maze.
Let us bow our heads,
And pray.
"Dear Heavenly Father,
We come to You today,
We ask You ever so humbly,
To guide our way.
For we can see far,
But not further than,
We can stray.

I ask You to pave the pieces,
On this road that I stay.
In Jesus mighty name I pray"
-Amen

# Recognition

I made it out the hood.
Where's my respect?
I made it out before
The negativity could infect.
I praise God,
I'm the one
That He selects.
I'm still learning
Excuse da slang,
In my dialect.
I know I'm growing,
It ain't my time yet.
But why you got to speak to me
Like I just learned the alphabet.
Talk to me like an intellect.
I may be 5'3,
But I got a growth mindset.
Big on mentality.
Knowledge my biggest asset.
Look past the physicality,

All you gonna see
Is me,
In a silhouette.
For the times
They didn't believe me.
So I left them in debt,
Think in depth.

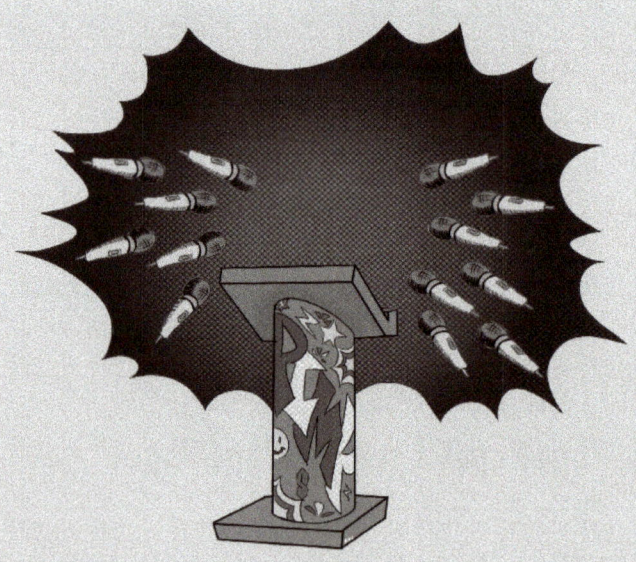

## 1%

Society is crazy.
Filled with everything.
It amazes me.
You can have down to earth
Mud brothers.
Or people who tear you down
For the fuck of it.
Tell me what do you gain?
You lost profit.
Don't say my name in vain.
I am the lost Prophet.
We're in the same environment,
But I'm a different product.
I got talent.
This isn't luck.
I turned my pain into passion,
I was the star who got struck.
I'm on the way out the smuck.
Quick to knuck,
If you buck.
I don't give a fuck.

I got nothing to lose,
Ain't shit I'm giving up.
I can stoop down to your level,
I know I'll rise back up.
Dancing with the devil,
I'll never slip up.
Get me out the group,
This staff is corrupt.
Fuck all the taxes they deduct.
I want to be in the 1%.
So, my cash won't be interrupt.
My kind never gets chosen.
We were never plucked.
Unless for sports or a publicity
stunt.
The government is my enemy,
The ones I shall confront.
To fight for my freedom,
To get the life I truly want.

## Congratulations

We are gathered here for a
celebration.
To celebrate the elevation.
All the time that took with
dedication.
All the days spent with
anticipation.
To pursue an education.
Days during the journey,
Feels like isolation.
Constant deadlines became
constant situations.
Phone calls to God asking for
salvation.
Sometimes it's hard to even
stand in formation.
That's when God kick in with the
motivation.
Putting you back in full rotation.
Breaking out the limits in

limitation.
No matter the time it took from
the duration.
Even if you had to step away for
a lil vacation.
Take a lil break,
Call it hydration.
God was transforming you into a
new location.
As we're all here for this special
occasion,
I say welcome,
To your graduation.

# Post-Graduation

# **Path of Righteousness**

Through my walk in the valley of
the shadow of death.
I can feel a sense of intuition,
From the center of my chest.
Whispers of insights,
Leading me to be the best.
Every day I shall fight,
Because this is a retest.
Success makes you a warrior,
My one only quest.
I shall never compare,
This ain't no contest.
I don't even say I'm lucky to be
here,
Because I'm blessed.
I don't manifest,
That didn't do shit,
When I was stressed.
With God all it took was just one
confess.

Passive income,
Simply a reinvest.
Back where I'm from,
He's the reason we progress.

# Poetic Journey

Walking through the valley
Of my poetic journey.
Feelin' like I'm at the steps,
How I'm still learning.
I was stuck in pain,
I was yearning.
I was walking in the rain,
It was burning.
I had lost what I had gained,
No returning.
I'm still walking with
Discernment.
Lost my mind,
No telling where it went.
Speaking out dollars,
While I try to make cents.
My mind's getting tense,
Show me how to dispense.
I just need a lil guidance.

Spent too much time on the
fence.
I want to be booked for events.
I want to be the face that'll
represent,
For the present, future, and past
tense.
I'm spitting this shit,
It don't even make sense.
You can't even smell me,
I carry no scent
Lil Youngin,
Within my words,
Imma royal prince.
Sign my posts with incense,
Pimpin' in My Palace.

# **Dear Mom**

I know you tried to give me
The life I want.
Sometimes it's better to leave
that to me.
Mom
I appreciate the life you gave me
that I need.
Even if it was rough,
I made it out like Creed.
Tough nights you didn't cook,
I was too cramped to look,
You dug into your purse to get
your card.
My in the midst thoughts,
"You work too hard."
Seeing you hurt,
Has made me scarred.
In my thoughts I sit and sink.
Empty bowls in the kitchen sink,
That was earlier from me.

When I was once hungry.
Now I'm wondering,
How I can make mad money?
To bless my mommy,
For all her worry.
It's my reason on this land
In all honesty.

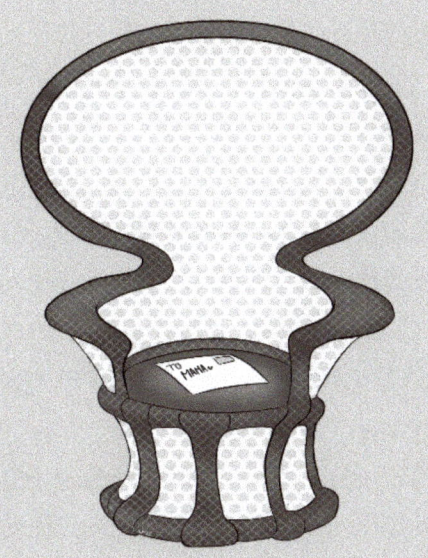

I am the one.
I am the third son.
I'm still the one.
I have it planned out.
I already won.
The race isn't done.
I'm still young.
I don't care about the fun.
I want to stack funds.
I want something I can
Pass on to my son.
I want wealth to run in my
family.
I want my family wealth to run. I
want to be honored to say
"I never had to pick up a gun,
I did it steadily and I won."
"All clean money, no dirty
ones."
"When money works for you,
that's how you know you're truly
done."
I'm ready for that time,
I've been working a ton.

## LLC

Fuck a 9-5,
That shift won't me.
I work 10-3,
Fuck being tied to a company.
It's PIMP Publishing!

## River Rock

God help us all.
Through our day,
Guide us, so we don't fall.
As we walk on our way,
I'm not worried about the
money.
For the debt is already paid.
I just want to say thank You &
Give You praise.
With my eyes closed
And my head laid.
I thank You for gathering me up,
out that place.
That dark empty space.
You were my guiding light
throughout the haze.
Stepping out the fight as I
finished the maze.
The only thing I can truly say,
The Lord works in mysterious
ways.

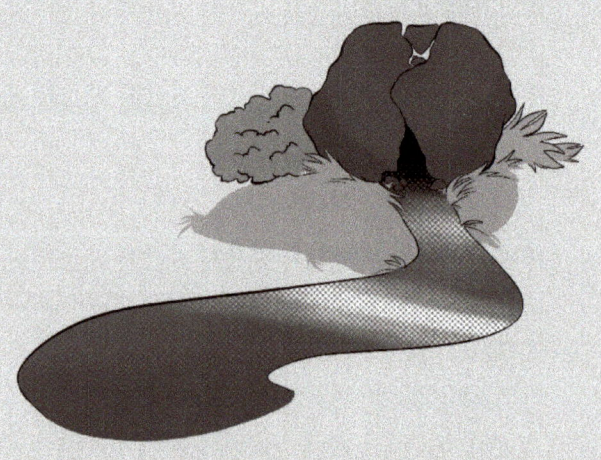

## On a Come Up

I am a poet.
Imma Poet,
You gonna fo sho know it.
Make you look through my
eyes,
How I show it.
Read throughout my life,
As I quote it.
Feel what I say;
Like clay,
How I mold it.
I'm going for the gold.
Until then,
I won't quit.
I'm running 'til I'm old.
I'm a D1 Commit
This the title I own.
PIMP